Kate & Pippin

An Unlikely Love Story

Martin Springett

Photographs by **Isobel Springett**

 PUFFIN

The fawn lay still and quiet. She was alone and afraid as she waited for her mother to come back.

Every little deer needs its mother to protect it from the many dangers of the forest.

But her mother did not return, and three long days passed.

Finally, as the hungry fawn cried, friendly hands lifted her up.

They gently carried her away from the field where she had been hiding and brought her to a nearby house.

Kate, a Great Dane, was asleep on her comfy round bed when she felt a small, warm presence.

She was surprised to see a fawn lying beside her!

Kate gave the young deer a nuzzle and a lick.

The fawn was certain she had found a
new mother. She snuggled in close to Kate
and gave a soft cry.

Kate had never had puppies of her own.
But she was a gentle dog, and being a mom
to the little deer came naturally.

Watching them together,
Kate's owner, Isobel, realized
the fawn might be staying
with them for a while and
would need a name.

Isobel decided on Pippin—
the sound of the name suited
the tiny deer perfectly.

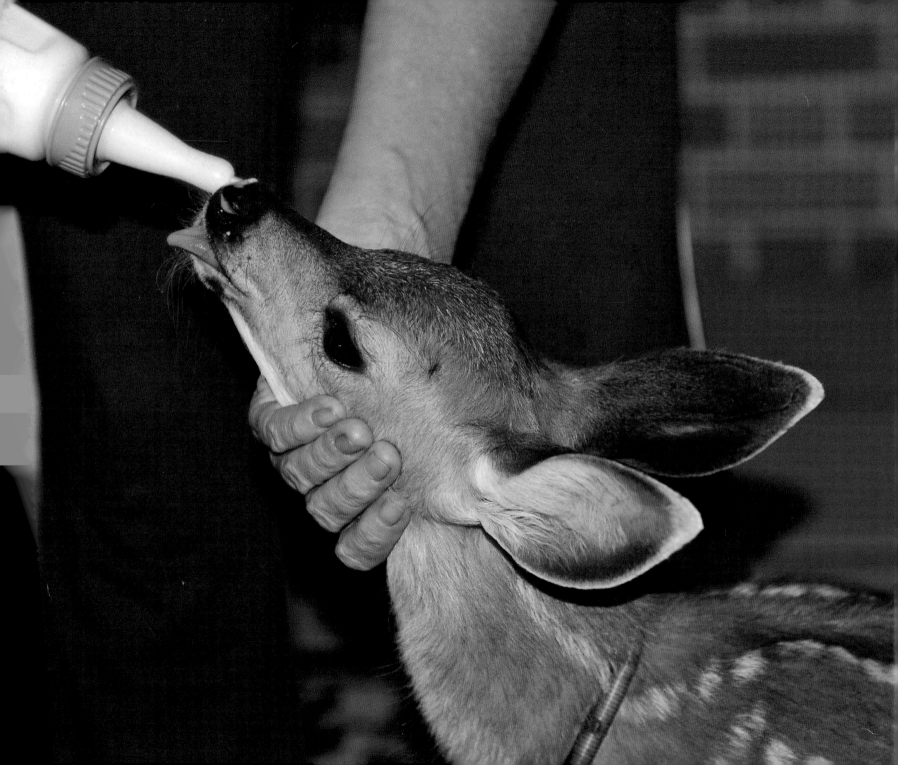

Even though she was hungry, Pippin didn't know what to make of the baby bottle that Isobel offered her.

At first she bit the bottle, and she was disappointed when she couldn't get at the sheep's milk inside.

Gradually she calmed down and began to suck. After two days of practice, Pippin was feeding contentedly.

As Pippin grew, her bond with Kate also grew. She followed the big black dog everywhere, just as a puppy would follow its mother.

After a week indoors, gaining strength and confidence, Pippin took her first steps outside. She made her way to the short set of stairs that led to the garden.

The stairs were a
challenge for the fawn,
but she eventually
stepped down onto
the grass.

Outside, Kate and Pippin began to play!
They rolled around on the lawn and chased
each other, running and leaping everywhere.
Then they returned to the house to sleep.

One evening, though, the fawn
did not return to the house.
Isobel called to her, and Kate
waited patiently for her to come
home, but she had disappeared
into the forest.

Kate and Isobel worried they
might never see Pippin again.

They were both up early the next morning, waiting.

Finally, at the edge of the trees, the long grass rustled and Pippin came into view! She trotted up to Kate and made a little greeting sound before asking to be fed.

From then on, Pippin slept in the forest each night but came back almost every morning. She loved to run around the farm, playing with her mom and enjoying snacks from Isobel, like bananas and bread.

Pippin grew up
quickly, but she was
still Kate's little pup.

She made other animal friends, too, including Henry the cat, who had lived with Kate for many years.

Henry did not want a bath every time she visited, but he let Pippin clean him with her long pink tongue.

Pippin gradually became an independent deer. She no longer needed to be bottle-fed, and she foraged on plants and grasses in the forest.

But even when she was fully grown, Pippin always came back to the farm to play with Kate.

Sometimes, Pippin still invites herself into the house for a visit. Pippin is a wild animal and the forest is her home, but she and Kate remain the best of friends.

This book is for our mother, Joan Springett.

PUFFIN CANADA

Published by the Penguin Group

Penguin Group (Canada), 90 Eglinton Avenue East, Suite 700, Toronto, Ontario, Canada M4P 2Y3
(a division of Pearson Canada Inc.)

Penguin Group (USA) Inc., 375 Hudson Street, New York, New York 10014, U.S.A.
Penguin Books Ltd, 80 Strand, London WC2R 0RL, England
Penguin Ireland, 25 St Stephen's Green, Dublin 2, Ireland (a division of Penguin Books Ltd)
Penguin Group (Australia), 250 Camberwell Road, Camberwell, Victoria 3124 Australia (a division
of Pearson Australia Group Pty Ltd)
Penguin Books India Pvt Ltd, 11 Community Centre, Panchsheel Park, New Delhi – 110 017, India
Penguin Group (NZ), 67 Apollo Drive, Rosedale, Auckland 0632, New Zealand (a division of Pearson
New Zealand Ltd)
Penguin Books (South Africa) (Pty) Ltd, 24 Sturdee Avenue, Rosebank, Johannesburg 2196, South Africa

Penguin Books Ltd, Registered Offices: 80 Strand, London WC2R 0RL, England

Published in Puffin Canada hardcover by Penguin Group (Canada), a division of Pearson Canada Inc.,
2012. Simultaneously published in the U.S.A. by Henry Holt and Company, LLC, 175 Fifth Avenue,
New York, NY 10010.

10 9 8 7 6 5 4 3 2 1

Text copyright © Martin Springett, 2012
Photographs copyright © Isobel Springett, 2012

Designed by Elynn Cohen

Manufactured in the U.S.A.

Library and Archives Canada Cataloguing in Publication
Springett, Martin
Kate & Pippin : an unlikely love story / text by Martin Springett ; photos by Isobel Springett.
ISBN 978-0-670-06597-4

1. Great Dane—Pictorial works. 2. Fawns—Pictorial works. 3. Parental behavior in animals—Pictorial
works. I. Springett, Isobel II. Title. III. Title: Kate and Pippin.
SF429.G7S77 2012   636.73   C2011-907323-4

American Library of Congress Cataloging-in-Publication Data available

Visit the Penguin Group (Canada) website at **www.penguin.ca**

Special and corporate bulk purchase rates available; please see **www.penguin.ca/corporatesales**
or call 1-800-810-3104, ext. 2477